A Bad Day at Cherry Farm

CB134455

Written by Nadja Fisher
Illustrated by Adele Jackson

Without warning, huge hailstones hammered down from the sky. Anka and Miro ran outside carrying nets. The hailstones plopped on the ground or crashed into the cherry trees.

"Quick!" Mum shouted through the noise. "The nets over the trees have become too heavy, so we have to shake off the hailstones. We have to replace damaged nets, too. If we don't keep our trees covered, our harvest will be destroyed!"

Everyone on the farm was trying to protect the ripe fruit by shaking the heavy hailstones off the nets. They replaced nets that had been blown off or that had holes in them.

Minutes later, it was all over. The clouds parted. The sun came out. Everyone stood around, looking at the damage the hail had caused. Because the hailstones had been huge, most of the cherries were bruised.

"What do we do now?" Miro asked. "We were so close to the harvest. Now, the cherries are all damaged, so we can't sell them fresh anymore."

Dad gave Mum a worried look.

"We have to harvest them," Joan, who was the person in charge, said.

"Yes," Dad agreed. "We have to pick them as soon as we can. If we can't sell them, we will lose a lot of money."

The neighbours had heard about the disaster at Cherry Farm so they came to help harvest the cherries. They all grabbed containers. They strapped them around their shoulders. They spread out across the orchard.

It was getting dark when they finished. They all stood next to the ten huge bins filled with cherries.

“Let’s put the cherries in cold storage. We have to decide what to do with them,” Mum said.

“We want to thank you all for your help, so we are making a big dinner,” Dad announced. “I am making my famous nut roast!”

Everyone cheered.

After dinner, Dad gave Miro a piece of paper so he could write down all their ideas.

"Why don't we make the cherries into jam?" their neighbour, Hank, said. "Everyone loves jam. It would sell well at the market."

"I have a great recipe for cherry cheesecake. We could sell cheesecakes at our stall at the market," Dad added.

"I have a friend who works for a juice company. They are always looking for fresh fruit," Joan offered. "Because they make the fruit into juice, the fruit doesn't have to be perfect – just fresh."

"How about pureed cherries?" said Miro. "If we sell pureed cherries in jars, then people can use them for all sorts of desserts. They can add the puree to pies or eat it with cream."

"They all sound like great ideas!" said Mum. "We just need to do it all quickly while the fruit is still fresh. Otherwise, we won't be able to sell anything at all."

"Right," said Joan. "Let's go to bed, so we can get started bright and early. These cherries need to be used as soon as possible."

The next day, Mum gave Hank one bin so he could make jam. Dad gave Anka a list and they went to the shop to buy all the ingredients for the cheesecakes. Mum and Miro washed the cherries. Then, they took out the stones, so they could cook the cherries and puree them in the blender. Joan rang her friend at the juice company. She arranged for the company to pick up six of the bins. Then, she went to help Hank make jam.

By the weekend, eight bins were gone. The juice company had picked up six bins. Hank and Joan had used one bin to make 2,000 jars of jam. Dad and Anka had made 50 cheesecakes. Mum and Miro had pureed almost a whole bin of cherries. They had 500 containers of puree. They loaded it all onto the truck and drove to the market.

The market was busy, which meant they sold a lot. They even sold some jam to Stella, the owner of the fruit store. Because Stella liked the jam so much, she ordered an extra 5,000 jars for the store. Everyone was happy. They kept the last cheesecake so they could take it home to celebrate.

When they got home, they counted what they had left. They still had 1,000 jars of cherry jam.

"That's good," said Mum, "because we have only enough cherries to make an extra 4,000 jars of jam. So that gives us the 5,000 we need to give to the fruit store."

"Yes, but they were not such a good idea because they were a lot of work to make. We could not sell them for much money," Dad explained.

There were still 250 containers of pureed cherries. "The puree was cheap and easy to make," Mum said. "But it was not so popular, and as a result we didn't sell all the containers. Because we have containers left over, we will have to go back to the market next week to sell more."

"Good news," said Joan as she walked in. "My friend from the juice company gave me a call."

Everyone was looking at Joan now. "Since our cherries tasted so good, the juice company wanted to place an order for next year," she said. "We sold a lot at the market and we have an order from the shop and the juice company. As a result, we didn't make a big loss after all!"

"Great!" Anka whooped. "Now all we have to decide is if it is better to sell the cherries fresh to eat, or if we want to make jam and sell the cherries to the juice company instead."

"OK, let's go and eat some cheesecake and crunch some numbers, then," Mum smiled.